SELECTED POEMS

Revised and Expanded

By Charles Simic

What the Grass Says   (1967)
Somewhere Among Us a Stone Is Taking Notes   (1969)
Dismantling the Silence   (1971)
White   (1972)
Return to a Place Lit by a Glass of Milk   (1974)
Biography and a Lament   (1976)
Charon's Cosmology   (1977)
Classic Ballroom Dances   (1980)
Austerities   (1982)
Weather Forecast for Utopia and Vicinity   (1983)
Selected Poems   (1985)
Unending Blues   (1986)
The World Doesn't End   (1989)
The Book of Gods and Devils   (1990)
Selected Poems, Revised and Expanded   (1990)

Charles Simic

SELECTED POEMS

1963–1983

REVISED AND EXPANDED

GEORGE BRAZILLER

NEW YORK

Poems included in this selection have been previously
published in the following volumes:

DISMANTLING THE SILENCE, copyright © 1971 by
Charles Simic; originally published by George Braziller.

RETURN TO A PLACE LIT BY A GLASS OF MILK,
copyright © 1974 by Charles Simic;
originally published by George Braziller.

CHARON'S COSMOLOGY, copyright © 1977 by Charles
Simic; originally published by George Braziller.

WHITE, copyright © 1980 by Charles Simic;
originally published by Logbridge-Rhodes.

CLASSIC BALLROOM DANCES, copyright © 1980 by
Charles Simic; originally published by George Braziller.

AUSTERITIES, copyright © 1982 by Charles Simic;
originally published by George Braziller.

WEATHER FORECAST FOR UTOPIA & VICINITY
POEMS 1967–1982, copyright © 1980 by Charles Simic;
originally published by Station Hill Press.

The author wishes to thank the Ingram Merill Foundation
for support during the preparation of this book.

Published in the United States in 1990 by
George Braziller, Inc.

Library of Congress Cataloging in Publication Data

Simic, Charles, 1938–
Selected Poems, 1963–1983—Rev. and expanded
I. Title.
PS3569.14725A6   1990—dc20   89-25129
ISBN 0-8076-1240-5 paper

Text design by Joe Marc Freedman
Printed in the United States of America

CONTENTS

from

RETURN TO A PLACE LIT
BY A GLASS OF MILK
(1974)

from

WHITE
(1970-1980)

from

CHARON'S COSMOLOGY
(1977)

from

CLASSIC BALLROOM DANCES
(1980)

from

WEATHER FORECAST FOR UTOPIA AND VICINITY
(1967–1982)

from

AUSTERITIES
(1982)

Dismantling
the Silence

BUTCHER SHOP

Sometimes walking late at night
I stop before a closed butcher shop.
There is a single light in the store
Like the light in which the convict digs his tunnel.

An apron hangs on the hook:
The blood on it smeared into a map
Of the great continents of blood,
The great rivers and oceans of blood.

There are knives that glitter like altars
In a dark church
Where they bring the cripple and the imbecile
To be healed.

There is a wooden block where bones are broken,
Scraped clean—a river dried to its bed
Where I am fed,
Where deep in the night I hear a voice.

TAPESTRY

It hangs from heaven to earth.
There are trees in it, cities, rivers,
small pigs and moons. In one corner
the snow falling over a charging cavalry,
in another women are planting rice.

You can also see:
a chicken carried off by a fox,
a naked couple on their wedding night,
a column of smoke,
an evil-eyed woman spitting into a pail of milk.

What is behind it?
—Space, plenty of empty space.

And who is talking now?
—A man asleep under his hat.

What happens when he wakes up?
—He'll go into a barbershop.
They'll shave his beard, nose, ears and hair,
To make him look like everyone else.

EVENING

The snail gives off stillness.
The weed is blessed.
At the end of a long day
The man finds joy, the water peace.

Let all be simple. Let all stand still
Without a final direction.
That which brings you into the world
To take you away at death
Is one and the same;
The shadow long and pointy
Is its church.

At night some understand what the grass says.
The grass knows a word or two.
It is not much. It repeats the same word
Again and again, but not too loudly...

THE INNER MAN

It isn't the body
That's a stranger.
It's someone else.

We poke the same
Ugly mug
At the world.
When I scratch,
He scratches too.

There are women
Who claim to have held him.
A dog follows me about.
It might be his.

If I'm quiet, he's quieter.
So I forget him.
Yet, as I bend down
To tie my shoelaces,
He's standing up.

We cast a single shadow.
Whose shadow?

I'd like to say:
"He was in the beginning
And he'll be in the end,"
But one can't be sure.

At night
As I sit
Shuffling the cards of our silence,
I say to him:

"Though you utter
Every one of my words,
You are a stranger.
It's time you spoke."

PASTORAL

I came to a meadow
Where the grass was silence
And the flowers
Words

I saw the blossoms
Were of flesh and blood
And that they tremble and fear
The wind like a knife

So sat I between the word *truth*
And the word *fable*
Took out my empty bowl
And spoon

Asked both about *love*
In the silence
With the night falling
Heard her call my name

Spat in the palms of my hands
To catch stars in them
Like fireflies
And light her way to me

FEAR

Fear passes from man to man
Unknowing,
As one leaf passes its shudder
To another.

All at once the whole tree is trembling
And there is no sign of the wind.

MARCHING

After I forgot about the horses
And when the fire turned into cool water flowing,
And the old woman took off her mourning to enter a coffin
At the end of a long life

A horse stood like an apparition,
A dream of a drowned girl cast out by the sea,
Suddenly he turned his head, bugler turning his bugle
To face the moon shining like a newlaid egg.

Then I rose in my house among my sons,
I put on my old clothes and my muddy boots,
My clothes smelling of wolves and deep snow,
My boots that have trodden men's faces.

I remembered the swamps, grass taller than horses,
Fast rivers softer than haylofts,
Where I'll stumble into deep hollows, dark eyelids,
Until I am buried under human droppings.

Blood rose into my head shaking its little bells.
In the valley the glow died in the udder of the cow.
The trees ceased playing with their apples
And the wind brought the sound of men marching.

A dog went along the road in front of marching soldiers,
A man who was to be hanged went along the road,
His head was bent, his face was dark and twisted
As if death meant straining to empty one's bowels.

So close the doors and windows and do not look,
The stars will come into the autumn sky
Like boats looking for survivors at sea
But no son of yours will rise from the deep.

CHORUS FOR ONE VOICE

I'm going to lie down next to you.
It cannot grow colder than this hour.
Strange men are gathered again
Drinking and singing. A different young man
Sits in their midst dressed in a uniform.

We are well into the night. Black moon.
With candle and spoon they examine its mouth
A man with dead soul and dog-licked knuckles
Eats from a paper plate.

I'm going to lie down next to you
As if nothing has happened:
Boot, shoemaker's knife, woman,
Your point bearing to my heart's true north.

◆

This is a tale with a kernel.
You'll have to use your own teeth to crack it.

If not tonight, well then . . . tomorrow.
Who keeps a clear head,
Who doesn't take a nap . . .
There isn't much choice anyway,
It's too late to get your money back.

All I can say at this point—
You won't have to kiss anyone's ass,
Nor will you have to sign anything.
It will all take place on the quiet
The way love is made.

◆

A sound of wings doesn't mean there's a bird.
If you've eaten today, no reason to think you'll eat
    tomorrow.
People can also be processed into soap.
The trees rustle. There's not always someone to answer
    them.
Moon hound of the north you come barking you come
    barking.
It's not only its own life that man's body has to endure.

◆

WANTED: A needle swift enough
To sew this poem into a blanket.

PSALM

1

Old ones to the side.

If there's a tailor, let him sit
With his legs crossed.
My suit will arrive in a moment.

All priests into mouse-holes.
All merchants into pigs. We'll cut their throats later.

To the beggars a yawn,
We'll see how they'll climb into it.

To the one who thinks, to the one between yes and no,
A pound of onions to peel.

To the mad ones crowns, if they still want them.
To the soldier a manual to turn into a flea.

No one is to touch the children
No one is to shovel out the dreamers.

2

I'm Joseph of the Joseph of the Joseph who rode on
    a donkey,
A wind-mill on the tongue humming with stars,
Columbus himself chained to a chair,
I'm anyone looking for a broom-closet.

3

You must understand that I write this at night
Their sleep surrounds me like an ocean.
Her name is Mary, the most mysterious of all.
She's a forest, standing at the beginning of time.
I'm someone lying within it. This light is our sperm.
The forest is old, older than sleep,
Older than this psalm I'm making up as I go.

POEM

Every morning I forget how it is.
I watch the smoke mount
In great strides above the city.
I belong to no one.

Then, I remember my shoes,
How I have to put them on,
How bending over to tie them up
I will look into the earth.

SUMMER MORNING

I love to stay in bed
All morning,
Covers thrown off, naked,
Eyes closed, listening.

Outside they are opening
Their primers
In the little school
Of the corn field.

There's a smell of damp hay,
Of horses, laziness,
Summer sky and eternal life.

I know all the dark places
Where the sun hasn't reached yet,
Where the last cricket
Has just hushed; anthills
Where it sounds like it's raining;
Slumbering spiders spinning wedding dresses.

I pass over the farmhouses
Where the little mouths open to suck,
Barnyards where a man, naked to the waist,
Washes his face and shoulders with a hose,
Where the dishes begin to rattle in the kitchen.

The good tree with its voice
Of a mountain stream
Knows my steps.
It, too, hushes.

I stop and listen:
Somewhere close by
A stone cracks a knuckle,
Another rolls over in its sleep.

I hear a butterfly stirring
Inside a caterpillar,
I hear the dust talking
Of last night's storm.

Further ahead, someone
Even more silent
Passes over the grass
Without bending it.

And all of a sudden!
In the midst of that quiet,
It seems possible
To live simply on this earth.

DISMANTLING THE SILENCE

Take down its ears first,
Carefully, so they don't spill over.
With a sharp whistle slit its belly open.
If there are ashes in it, close your eyes
And blow them whichever way the wind is pointing.
If there's water, sleeping water,
Bring the root of a flower that hasn't drunk for a month.

When you reach the bones,
And you haven't got a dog with you,
And you haven't got a pine coffin
And a cart pulled by oxen to make them rattle,
Slip them quickly under your skin.
Next time you hunch your shoulders
You'll feel them pressing against your own.

It is now pitch dark.
Slowly and with patience
Search for its heart. You will need
To crawl far into the empty heavens
To hear it beat.

BESTIARY FOR THE FINGERS OF MY RIGHT HAND

1

Thumb, loose tooth of a horse.
Rooster to his hens.
Horn of a devil. Fat worm
They have attached to my flesh
At the time of my birth.
It takes four to hold him down,
Bend him in half, until the bone
Begins to whimper.

Cut him off. He can take care
Of himself. Take root in the earth,
Or go hunting with wolves.

2

The second points the way.
True way. The path crosses the earth,
The moon and some stars.
Watch, he points further.
He points to himself.

3

The middle one has backache.
Stiff, still unaccustomed to this life;
An old man at birth. It's about something
That he had and lost,
That he looks for within my hand,
The way a dog looks
For fleas
With a sharp tooth.

4

The fourth is mystery.
Sometimes as my hand
Rests on the table
He jumps by himself
As though someone called his name.

After each bone, finger,
I come to him, troubled.

5

Something stirs in the fifth
Something perpetually at the point
Of birth. Weak and submissive,
His touch is gentle.
It weighs a tear.
It takes the mote out of the eye.

FORK

This strange thing must have crept
Right out of hell.
It resembles a bird's foot
Worn around the cannibal's neck.

As you hold it in your hand,
As you stab with it into a piece of meat,
It is possible to imagine the rest of the bird:
Its head which like your fist
Is large, bald, beakless and blind.

SPOON

An old spoon,
Chewed,
Licked clean,

Polished back
To its evil-eyed
Glow,

Eying you now
From the table,
Ready to scratch

Today's date
And your name
On the bare wall.

KNIFE

1

Father-confessor
Of the fat hen
On the red altar
Of its throat,

A tongue,
All alone,
Bringing the darkness of a mouth
Now lost.

A single shining eye
Of a madman—
If there's a tear in it,
Who is it for?

2

It is a candle
It is also a track
Of crooked letters;
The knife's mysterious writings.

We go down
An inner staircase.
We walk under the earth.
The knife lights the way.

Through bones of animals,
Water, beard of a wild boar—
We go through stones, embers,
We are after a scent.

3

So much darkness
Everywhere.
We are in a bag
Slung
Over someone's shoulders.

You hear the sound
Of marching boots.
You hear the earth
Answering
With a hollow thud.

If it's a poem
You want,
Take a knife;

A star of solitude,
It will rise and set in your hand.

MY SHOES

Shoes, secret face of my inner life:
Two gaping toothless mouths,
Two partly decomposed animal skins
Smelling of mice-nests.

My brother and sister who died at birth
Continuing their existence in you,
Guiding my life
Toward their incomprehensible innocence.

What use are books to me
When in you it is possible to read
The Gospel of my life on earth
And still beyond, of things to come?

I want to proclaim the religion
I have devised for your perfect humility
And the strange church I am building
With you as the altar.

Ascetic and maternal, you endure:
Kin to oxen, to Saints, to condemned men,
With your mute patience, forming
The only true likeness of myself.

AX

Whoever swings an ax
Knows the body of man
Will again be covered with fur.
The stench of blood and swamp water
Will return to its old resting place.
They'll spend their winters
Sleeping like the bears.
The skin on the breasts of their women
Will grow coarse. He who cannot
Grow teeth, will not survive.
He who cannot howl
Will not find his pack . . .

These dark prophecies were gathered,
Unknown to myself, by my body
Which understands historical probabilities,
Lacking itself, in its essence, a future.

STONE

Go inside a stone
That would be my way.
Let somebody else become a dove
Or gnash with a tiger's tooth.
I am happy to be a stone.

From the outside the stone is a riddle:
No one knows how to answer it.
Yet within, it must be cool and quiet
Even though a cow steps on it full weight,
Even though a child throws it in a river;
The stone sinks, slow, unperturbed
To the river bottom
Where the fishes come to knock on it
And listen.

I have seen sparks fly out
When two stones are rubbed,
So perhaps it is not dark inside after all;
Perhaps there is a moon shining
From somewhere, as though behind a hill—
Just enough light to make out
The strange writings, the star-charts
On the inner walls.

POEM WITHOUT A TITLE

I say to the lead
Why did you let yourself
Be cast into a bullet?
Have you forgotten the alchemists?
Have you given up hope
Of turning into gold?

Nobody answers.
Lead. Bullet.
With names like that
The sleep is deep and long.

EXPLORERS

They arrive inside
The object at evening.
There's no one to greet them.

The lamps they carry
Cast their shadows
Back into their own minds.

They write in their journals:

The sky and the earth
Are of the same impenetrable color.
If there are rivers and lakes,
They must be under the ground.
Of the marvels we sought, no trace.
Of the strange new stars, nothing.
There's not even wind or dust,
So we must conclude that someone
Passed recently with a broom...

As they write, the new world
Gradually stitches
Its black thread into them.

Eventually nothing is left
Except a low whisper
Which might belong
Either to one of them
Or to someone who came before.

It says: "I'm happy
We are finally all here...

Let's make this our home."

CONCERNING MY NEIGHBORS,
THE HITTITES

Great are the Hittites.
Their ears have mice and mice have holes.
Their dogs bury themselves and leave the bones
To guard the house. A single weed holds all their storms
Until the spiderwebs spread over the heavens.
There are bits of straw in their lakes and rivers
Looking for drowned men. When a camel won't pass
Through the eye of one of their needles,
They tie a house to its tail. Great are the Hittites.
Their fathers are in cradles, their newborn make war.
To them lead floats, a leaf sinks. Their god is the size
Of a mustard seed so that he can be quickly eaten.

They also piss against the wind,
Pour water in a leaky bucket,
Strike two tears to make fire,
And have tongues with bones in them,
Bones of a wolf gnawed by lambs.

◆

They are also called mound-builders,
They are called Asiatic horses
That will drink on the Rhine, they are called
My grandmother's fortune telling, they are called
You can't take it to the grave with you.

It's that hum in your left ear,
A sigh coming from deep within you,
A dream in which you keep falling forever,
The hour in which you sit up in bed
As though someone has shouted your name.

No one knows why the Hittites exist,
Still, when two are whispering
One of them is listening.

Did they catch the falling knife?
They caught it like a fly with closed mouths.
Did they balance the last egg?
They struck the egg with a bone so it won't howl.
Did they wait for dead man's shoes?
The shoes went in at one ear and out the other.
Did they wipe the blood from their mousetraps?
They burnt the blood to warm themselves.
Are they cold with no pockets in their shrouds?
If the sky falls they shall have clouds for supper.

What do they have for us
To put in our pipes and smoke?
They have the braid of a beautiful girl
That drew a team of cattle
And the engraving of him who slept
With dogs and rose with fleas
Searching for its trace in the sky.

♦

And so there are fewer and fewer of them now.
Who wrote their name on paper
And burnt the paper? Who put snake-bones
In their pillows? Who threw nail-parings
In their soup? Who made them walk
Under the ladder? Who stuck pins
In their snapshots?

The wart of warts and his brother evil-eye.
Bone-lazy and her sister rabbit's-foot.
Cross-your-fingers and their father dogstar.
Knock-on-wood and his mother hell-fire.

Because the tail can't wag the cow.
Because the woods can't fly to the dove.
Because the stones haven't said their last word.
Because dunghills rise and empires fall.

◆

They are leaving behind
All the silver spoons
Found inside their throats at birth,
A hand they bit because it fed them,
Two rats from a ship that is still sinking,
A collection of various split hairs,
The leaf they turned over too late.

◆

All that salt cast over the shoulder,
All that bloody meat travelling under the saddles
      of nomads . . .

Here comes a forest in wolf's clothing,
The wise hen bows to the umbrella.

When the bloodshot evening meets the bloodshot night,
They tell each other bloodshot tales.

That bare branch over them speaks louder than words.
The moon is worn threadbare.

I repeat: lean days don't come singly,
It takes all kinds to make the sun rise.

The night is each man's castle.
Don't let the castle out of the bag.

Wind in the valley, wind in the high hills,
Practice will make this body fit this bed.

♦

May all roads lead
Out of a sow's ear
To what's worth
Two in the bush.

INVENTION OF NOTHING

I didn't notice
while I wrote here
that nothing remains of the world
except my table and chair.

And so I said:
(for the hell of it, to abuse patience)
Is this the tavern
without a glass, wine or waiter
where I'm the long awaited drunk?

The color of nothing is blue.
I strike it with my left hand and the hand disappears.
Why am I so quiet then
and so happy?

I climb on the table
(the chair is gone already)
I sing through the throat
of an empty beer-bottle.

errata

Where it says snow
read teeth-marks of a virgin
Where it says knife read
you passed through my bones
like a police-whistle
Where it says table read horse
Where it says horse read my migrant's bundle
Apples are to remain apples
Each time a hat appears
think of Isaac Newton
reading the Old Testament
Remove all periods
They are scars made by words
I couldn't bring myself to say
Put a finger over each sunrise
it will blind you otherwise
That damn ant is still stirring
Will there be time left to list
all errors to replace
all hands guns owls plates
all cigars ponds woods and reach
that beer-bottle my greatest mistake
the word I allowed to be written
when I should have shouted
her name

Return to
a Place Lit by
a Glass of Milk

THE BIRD

A bird calls me
From a dark tree
In my dream.

Calls me from the pink twig of daylight,
From the long shadow
That grows each day closer to my heart.
Calls me from the ends of the earth.

I give her my dreams.
She dyes them red.
I give her my breath.
She turns it into rustling leaves.

She calls me from the throne of the rising sun.
Her chirp like a match flickering
On a dark and windy threshold.

♦

Bird, shaped
Like the insides
Of a yawning
Mouth,

At five in the morning
When the sky turns clear and lucent
Like the water in which
They baptized a small child.

I started on the staircase
Of your song,
Naked,
Climbing like wood smoke.

The earth grew smaller underneath
My bare feet stood
At the crossroads
Where night and day meet,

Their fierce cold
Chilled me
To the bone.

♦

Later, I fell
In a clearing
In a dark, silent
Forest,

And dreamt I had
The eyes and ears
Of that bird
Watching me sleep.

ELEMENTARY
COSMOGONY

How to the invisible
I hired myself to learn
Whatever trade it might
Consent to teach me.

How the invisible
Came out for a walk
On a certain evening
Casting the shadow of a man.

How I followed behind
Dragging my body
Which is my tool box,
Which is my music box,

For a long apprenticeship
That has as its last
And seventh rule:
The submission to chance.

TWO RIDDLES

Hangs by a thread—
Whatever it is. Stripped naked.
Shivering. Human. Mortal.
On a thread finer than starlight.

By a power of a feeling,
Hangs, impossible, unthinkable,
Between the earth and the sky.
I, it says. I. I.

And how it boasts,
That everything that is to be known
About the wind
Is being revealed to it as it hangs.

◆

It goes without saying . . .
What does? No one knows.
Goes mysterious, ah funereal,
Goes for the hell of it.

If it has an opinion,
It keeps it to itself.
If it brings tidings,
It plays dumb, plays dead.

No use trying to pin it down.
It's elusive, of a retiring habit,
In a hurry of course, scurrying—
A blink of an eye and it's gone.

All that's known about it,
Is that it goes goes
Without saying.

BROOMS

for Tomaz, Susan and George

1

Only brooms
Know the devil
Still exists,

That the snow grows whiter
After a crow has flown over it,
That a dark dusty corner
Is the place of dreamers and children,

That a broom is also a tree
In the orchard of the poor,
That a hanging roach there
Is a mute dove.

2

Brooms appear in dreambooks
As omens of approaching death.
This is their secret life.
In public, they act like flat-chested old maids
Preaching temperance.

They are sworn enemies of lyric poetry.
In prison they accompany the jailer,
Enter cells to hear confessions.
Their short-end comes down
When you least expect it.

Left alone behind a door
Of a condemned tenement,
They mutter to no one in particular,
Words like *virgin wind moon-eclipse*,
And that most sacred of all names:
Hieronymous Bosch.

3

In this and in no other manner
Was the first ancestral broom made:
Namely, they plucked all the arrows
From the bent back of Saint Sebastian.
They tied them with a rope
On which Judas hung himself.
Stuck in the stilt
On which Copernicus
Touched the morning star . . .

Then the broom was ready
To leave the monastery.
The dust welcomed it—
That great pornographer
Immediately wanted to
Look under its skirt.

4

The secret teaching of brooms
Excludes optimism, the consolation
Of laziness, the astonishing wonders
Of a glass of aged moonshine.

It says: the bones end up under the table.
Bread-crumbs have a mind of their own.
The milk is you-know-who's semen.
The mice have the last squeal.

As for the famous business
Of levitation, I suggest remembering:
There is only one God
And his prophet is Mohammed.

5

And then finally there's your grandmother
Sweeping the dust of the nineteenth century
Into the twentieth, and your grandfather plucking
A straw out of the broom to pick his teeth.

Long winter nights.
Dawns a thousand years deep.
Kitchen windows like heads
Bandaged for toothache.

The broom beyond them sweeping,
Tucking in the lucent grains of dust
Into neat pyramids,
That have tombs in them,

Already sacked by robbers,
Once, long ago.

WATERMELONS

Green Buddhas
On the fruit stand.
We eat the smile
And spit out the teeth.

WATCH REPAIR

A small wheel
Incandescent,
Shivering like
A pinned butterfly.

Hands thrown up
In all directions:
The crossroads
One arrives at
In a nightmare.

Higher than that
Number 12 presides
Like a beekeeper
Over the swarming honeycomb
Of the open watch.

Other wheels
That could fit
Inside a raindrop.

Tools
That must be splinters
Of arctic starlight.

Tiny golden mills
Grinding invisible
Coffee beans.

When the coffee's boiling
Cautiously,
So it doesn't burn us,
We raise it
To the lips
Of the nearest
Ear.

TRAVELLING

I turn myself into a sack.
An old ragpicker
Takes me out at dawn.
We go shuffling, we go stooped.

Here he says is the blue tie,
A man climbed it as it hung from his neck.
He's up there sobbing now
For he doesn't know how to come down.

But I say nothing, what can a sack say?

Here he says is the overcoat.
His name is Ahab, his tatters are our tatters.
He is searching for the tailor who made him.
He wants all his black threads ripped out.

But I say nothing, what can a sack say?

Here he says are the boots,
As they sunk, as they went under
They saw their lives in a flash,
They'll cling to us wherever we go.

But I say nothing, what can a sack
Stuffed to its throat say?

BALLAD

What's that approaching like dusk like poverty
A little girl picking flowers in a forest
The migrants' campfire of her long hair
Harm's way she comes and the smile's round about way

In another life in another life
Aunt rain sewing orphan's buttons to each pebble
Solitude's dark stitch
Let your horns out devil stone

Screendoor screeching in the wind
Mother-hobble-gobble baking apples
Wooden spoon dancing—ah the idyllic life of wooden
    spoons
I need a feast table to spread my memories on

Lone little girl fishing using me as bait
Me a gloomy woodcutter in the forest of words
I'm going to say one thing and mean another
I'll tuck you in a matchbox like a hornet

In that other life in that other life
Dandelion and red poppy grow in my back yard
Shoes in the rain bark at the milkman
Little girl playing blindman's bluff

The words are playing too—
You are *it* she says laughing and is gone
Divination by the sound of one's own heartbeat
Draw near to what doesn't say yes or no

And she had nothing under her dress
Star like an eye the fighting cocks have overlooked
Tune up your fingers and whistle
On forest path she hides herself behind a tree

I walk the way you vanished by spellbound
Not even the wind blew to remind me of time
Approachs that which they insist on calling happiness
The nightbird says its name

On your arms raised high hoist this vision
Some evening when they come to quiz you in love
Glancing back under the dark trees
Little girl skipping the owls' hushed way

SOLVING THE RIDDLE

The cloud's a clue. O cloud!
Two elm trees looking suspicious.

Whose clues. My clues,
All my cheating clues,
All my grumpy omens,
It's time we solve this riddle.

Mr. Clue sits.
Mr. Omen flaps his wings.
They make one hand unearn
What the other earns.

♦

I have a feud with my lifeline.
I take note of its crossroads and ditches.
I travel crucified.

I go solving with my ears.
The ears hear what's not there.
I go solving with my eyes.
The eyes see nothing. The eyes see everything.

♦

Round, round
So that it rolls easily away,
Rolls laughing
Shedding its skins, its pretty doll's dresses.

White, so that it hides
Cleverly in this paper,
And I believe it lost,
I believe it never was.

Heavy, so that I feel
Its weight on my shoulders,
My back bent into a question mark,
My foot making its comma.

♦

What is it that was under my nose
And is no more?
Did it go home?
Did it find its old sweetheart?

Nothing here now
But the same old thing
Telling the same old story
At the kitchen table:

It'll be here tomorrow,
Newly disguised, hard to recognize.
I keep its bone.
I keep its chipped bowl.

◆

We wave goodby
My most precious clue and I.
Two question marks.
Two asses' ears.

Around a riddle
Which keeps changing its answer,
We made our pallet,
Stone for a pillow.

The night was long and dark.

Inside my wine bottle
I was constructing a lighthouse
While all the others
Were making sailing ships.

THE PLACE

They were talking about the war
The table still uncleared in front of them.
Across the way, the first window
Of the evening was already lit.
He sat, hunched over, quiet,
The old fear coming over him . . .
It grew darker. She got up to take the plate—
Now unpleasantly white—to the kitchen.
Outside in the fields, in the woods
A bird spoke in proverbs,
A Pope went out to meet Attila,
The ditch was ready for its squad.

BREASTS

I love breasts, hard
Full breasts, guarded
By a button.

They come in the night.
The bestiaries of the ancients
Which include the unicorn
Have kept them out.

Pearly, like the east
An hour before sunrise,
Two ovens of the only
Philosopher's stone
Worth bothering about.

They bring on their nipples
Beads of inaudible sighs,
Vowels of delicious clarity
For the little red schoolhouse of our mouths.

Elsewhere, solitude
Makes another gloomy entry
In its ledger, misery
Borrows another cup of rice.

They draw nearer: Animal
Presence. In the barn
The milk shivers in the pail.

I like to come up to them
From underneath, like a kid
Who climbs on a chair
To reach a jar of forbidden jam.

Gently, with my lips,
Loosen the button.
Have them slip into my hands
Like two freshly poured beer-mugs.

I spit on fools who fail to include
Breasts in their metaphysics,
Star-gazers who have not enumerated them
Among the moons of the earth . . .

They give each finger
Its true shape, its joy:
Virgin soap, foam
On which our hands are cleansed.

And how the tongue honors
These two sour buns,
For the tongue is a feather
Dipped in egg-yolk.

I insist that a girl
Stripped to the waist
Is the first and last miracle,

That the old janitor on his deathbed
Who demands to see the breasts of his wife
For one last time
Is the greatest poet who ever lived.

O my sweet yes, my sweet no,
Look, everyone is asleep on the earth.

Now, in the absolute immobility
Of time, drawing the waist
Of the one I love to mine,

I will tip each breast
Like a dark heavy grape
Into the hive
Of my drowsy mouth.

CHARLES SIMIC

Charles Simic is a sentence.
A sentence has a beginning and an end.

Is he a simple or compound sentence?
It depends on the weather,
It depends on the stars above.

What is the subject of the sentence?
The subject is your beloved Charles Simic.

How many verbs are there in the sentence?
Eating, sleeping and fucking are some of its verbs.

What is the object of the sentence?
The object, my little ones,
Is not yet in sight.

And who is writing this awkward sentence?
A blackmailer, a girl in love,
And an applicant for a job.

Will they end with a period or a question mark?
They'll end with an exclamation point and an ink spot.

SOLITUDE

There now, where the first crumb
Falls from the table
You think no one hears it
As it hits the floor

But somewhere already
The ants are putting on
Their Quakers' hats
And setting out to visit you.

THE POINT

This is the story
Afraid to go on.

This is the iron cradle
Of the stillness
That rocks the story
Afraid to go on.

How it regrets
The loss of its purity,
The madness of this
Single burnt consonant,

Which now sits,
Shy, solitary,
Among all these
White spaces.

♦

And it dreams,
The story afraid to go on.

In its dream it builds itself
In the shape
Of the gallows-tree.

When the gallows are completed,
It hangs by the neck
What's left of its dreamings.

Underneath, in the dirt
The shadow of its beginning
Comes to nibble
Its quivering feet.

♦

There's no point,
Says the story
Afraid to go on.

It's all a question
Of the mote
In your eye.

It watches
As you watch.

Perhaps this evening
Reflects its final blackness,
Reflects its final mourning

Before it dissolves
Into a tear?

♦

After its death
They opened the story
Afraid to go on.
And found nothing.

Inside nothing
They found a slip
Of the tongue.
Inside the tongue
A loose hair.
Inside the hair,
They found

Whatever
Is destroyed
Each time
It is named.

THE PILLOW

Are we still travelling?
Whiteness, you came out of a dog's mouth
On a cold day. Apron,
I lie within you like an apple.

You've lit up my forest. Two
Black winds you sell. Do you still
Guard me from robbers
On the road fearsome and lonesome?

To tie my breath inside you
Into a knot—find the way
Back to your old scent—
It still hasn't bought me a mockingbird.

We separated, sacred time.
I stretch between two chairs. Recently
I started wearing blinders. One-legged,
Since there's no room for the other.

The dead love eggs. This is
That stone tucked beneath you
Speaking. Bared now,
For those who grit their teeth in sleep

To lay down their heads.

THE SOUP

Take the lump in your throat,
And the hair standing on your head,
And your dirty feet,
And your cock and your fingernails.

The clock that goes to 13.
The bare room, the iron cot.
The cockroach of history running up the wall.

Instead of salt,
Laugh into it.
Instead of pepper,
Swear loudly.

Then wipe your red nose
On the black armband on your sleeve.

♦

The soup of fortune tellers,
Watchmakers, mirrormakers.
Steaming soup
Full of skulls and bones.

The soup of alchemists,
Pickpockets, fishermen for souls,
Widows, orphans and blind beggars.
The soup beloved by flies.

On what shall we cook it?

On the moustache of Joseph Stalin.
The fires of Treblinka.
The fires of Hiroshima.
The head of the condemned
The head swarming with memories.

Let's cook it until we raise
Our mothers' white bodies
Out of its murky depths.
They're huge, they are beautiful.
They're soaping themselves and laughing

◆

What do you think it will taste like?

Like spit on the dice.
Like barbed wire.
Like the black panties of Dulcinea of Toboso.
Like her toes painted red.
The angel riding a fat pig
Saying things in its ears
That make the pig blush.

At the end of a short, dark winter day,
We arouse the gods' curiosity
By ladling the soup of the world
Past our teeth.

◆

What shall we eat it with then?

With an old shoe left in the rain.
Two eyes quarreling in the same head.
The solitude of black wings.
The fish in the pet store aquarium that never sleeps.

We'll sit slurping
With our hats on:
A soup like forest of whispers,
A hearty slaughterhouse soup

◆

And this is what will have on the side:

The bread of memory, a black bread.
Cold wind fried in onions.
Blood sausages of yes and no.
A goose-roast of darkest thoughts.
A drop of milk from the Blessed Virgin's breast.

Columbus pissing at night in mid-Atlantic
With a sense of eternity.
That wine, that moonlight!
The sea and the sky like a wide-open mouth.

THE CHICKEN WITHOUT A HEAD

1

When two times two was three,
The chicken without a head was hatched.
When the earth was still flat,
It fell off its edge, daydreaming.
When there were 13 signs in the zodiac,
It found a dead star for its gizzard.
When the first fox was getting married,
It taught itself to fly with one wing.
When all the eggs were still golden,
The clouds in the sky tasted like sweet corn.
When the rain flooded its coop,
Its wishbone was its arc.
Ah, when the chicken had only itself to roast,
The lightning was its skewer,
The thunder its baste and salt.

2

The chicken without a head made a sigh,
And then a hailstone out of that sigh,
And the window for the hailstone to strike.
Nine lives it made for itself,
And nine coats of solitude to dress them in.
It made its own shadow. No, I'm lying.
It only made a flea to bite some holes in the shadow.
Made it all out of nothing. Made a needle
To sew back its broken eggshell.
Made the lovers naked. Everybody else put clothes
    on them.
Its father made the knife, but it polished the blade,

83

Until it threw back its image like a funhouse mirror.
Made it all out of raglets of time.
Who's to say it'd be happier if it didn't?

3

Hear the song of a chicken without a head
As it goes scratching in grave-dirt.
A song in which two parallel lines
Meet at infinity, in which God
Makes the last of the little apples,
In which golden fleece is heard growing
On a sad girl's pubis. The song
Of swearwords dreaming of a pure mouth.
The song of a doornail raised from the dead.
The song of circumspection because accomplices
Have been found, because the egg's safe
In the cuckoo's nest. The song
You wade into until your own hat floats.
A song of contagious laughter.
A lethal song.
That's right, the song of premonition.

4

On a headless evening of a headless day
The chicken on fire and the words
Around it like a ring of fabulous beasts.
Each night it threw them a bite-size portion of its heart.
The words were hungry, the night held the fork.
Whatever our stylish gallows-bird made, its head unmade,
Its long lost, axed-off sultan's head

Rose into the sky in a balloon of fiery numerals.
Down below the great feast went on:
The table that supplies itself with bread.
A saw that cuts a dream in half.
Wings so quick they don't get wet in heavy rain.
The egg that mutters to the frying pan:
I swear it by the hair in my yolk,
There's no such thing as a chicken without a head.

5

The chicken without a head ran a maze,
Ran half-plucked,
A serving fork stuck in its back,
Ran, backwards, into the blue of the evening.
Ran upsidedown,
Its drumsticks and talons in the clouds.
Someone huge and red-aproned rose in its wake.
Many black umbrellas parting to let it pass.
Ran leaving its squinting head far behind,
Its head reeking of barber's cologne.
Ran up the church steeple,
Up the lightning rod on that steeple
For the wind to hone its prettiest plumes.
Ran, and is still running this Good Friday,
Between raindrops,
Hellfoxes on its trail.

White

What is that little black thing I see there in the white?

Walt Whitman

WHITE

1

Out of poverty
To begin again:

With the color of the bride
And that of blindness,

Touch what I can
Of the quick,

Speak and then wait,
As if this light

Will continue to linger
On the threshold.

♦

All that is near,
I no longer give it a name.

Once a stone hard of hearing,
Once sharpened into a knife . . .

Now only a chill
Slipping through.

Enough glow to kneel by and ask
To be tied to its tail

When it goes marrying
Its cousins, the stars.

♦

Is it a cloud?
If it's a cloud it will move on.

The true shape of this thought,
Migrant, waning.

Something seeks someone,
It bears him a gift

Of himself, a bit
Of snow to taste,

Glimpse of his own nakedness
By which to imagine the face.

♦

On a late afternoon of snow
In a dim badly-aired grocery,

Where a door has just rung
With a short, shrill echo,

A little boy hands the old,
Hard-faced woman

Bending low over the counter,
A shiny nickel for a cupcake.

Now only that shine, now
Only that lull abides.

♦

That your gaze
Be merciful,

Sister, bride
Of my first hopeless insomnia.

Kind nurse, show me
The place of salves.

Teach me the song
That makes a man raise

His glass at dusk
Until a star dances in it.

♦

Who are you? Are you anybody
A moonrock would recognize?

There are words I need.
They are not near men.

I went searching.
Is this a deathmarch?

You bend me, bend me,
Oh toward what flower!

Little-known vowel,
Noose big for us all.

◆

As strange as a shepherd
In the Arctic Circle.

Someone like Bo-peep.
All his sheep are white

And he can't get any sleep
Over lost sheep.

And he's got a flute
Which says Bo-peep,

Which says Poor boy,
Take care of your snow-sheep.

                    to A.S. Hamilton
                    ◆

Then all's well and white,
And no more than white.

Illinois snowbound.
Indiana with one bare tree.

Michigan a storm-cloud.
Wisconsin empty of men.

There's a trap on the ice
Laid there centuries ago.

The bait is still fresh.
The metal glitters as the night descends.

♦

Woe, woe, it sings from the bough.
Our Lady, etc. . .

You had me hoodwinked.
I see your brand new claws.

Praying, what do I betray
By desiring your purity?

There are old men and women,
All bandaged up, waiting

At the spiked, wrought-iron gate
Of the Great Eye and Ear Infirmery.

♦

We haven't gone far . . .
Fear lives there too.

Five ears of my fingertips
Against the white page.

What do you hear?
We hear holy nothing

Blindfolding itself.
It touched you once, twice,

And tore like a stitch
Out of a new wound.

2

What are you up to son of a gun?
I roast on my heart's dark side.

What do you use as a skewer sweetheart?
I use my own crooked backbone.

What do you salt yourself with loverboy?
I grind the words out of my spittle.

And how will you know when you're done chump?
When the half-moons on my fingernails set.

With what knife will you carve yourself smartass?
The one I hide in my tongue's black boot.

•

Well, you can't call me a wrestler
If my own dead weight has me pinned down.

Well, you can't call me a cook
If the pot's got me under its cover.

Well, you can't call me a king
If the flies hang their hats in my mouth.

Well, you can't call me smart,
When the rain's falling my cup's in the cupboard.

Nor can you call me a saint,
If I didn't err, there wouldn't be these smudges.

♦

One has to manage as best as one can.
The poppies ate the sunset for supper.

One has to manage as best as one can.
Who stole my blue thread, the one

I tied around my pinky to remember?
One has to manage as best as one can.

The flea I was standing on, jumped.
One has to manage as best as one can.

I think my head went out for a walk.
One has to manage as best as one can.

♦

This is breath, only breath,
Think it over midnight!

A fly weighs twice as much.
The struck match nods as it passes,

But when I shout,
Its true name sticks in my throat.

It has to be cold
So the breath turns white,

And then mother, who's fast enough
To write his life on it?

♦

A song in prison
And for prisoners,

Made of what the condemned
Have hidden from the jailers.

White—let me step aside
So that the future may see you,

For when this sheet is blown away,
What else is left

But to set the food on the table,
To cut oneself a slice of bread?

♦

In an unknown year
Of an algebraic century,

An obscure widow
Wrapped in the colors of widowhood,

Met a true-blue orphan
On an indeterminate street-corner.

She offered him
A tiny sugar cube

In the hand so wizened
All the lines said: fate.

♦

Do you take this line
Stretching to infinity?

I take this chipped tooth
On which to cut it in half.

Do you take this circle
Bounded by a single curved line?

I take this breath
That it cannot capture.

Then you may kiss the spot
Where her bridal train last rustled.

♦

Winter can come now,
The earth narrow to a ditch—

And the sky with its castles and stone lions
Above the empty plains.

The snow can fall . . .
What other perennials would you plant,

My prodigals, my explorers
Tossing and turning in the dark

For those remote, finely honed bees,
The December stars?

◆

Had to get through me elsewhere.
Woe to bone

That stood in their way.
Woe to each morsel of flesh.

White ants
In a white anthill.

The rustle of their many feet
Scurrying—tiptoeing too.

Gravedigger ants.
Village-idiot ants.

◆

This is the last summoning.
Solitude—as in the beginning.

A zero burped by a bigger zero—
It's an awful licking I got.

And fear—that dead letter office.
And doubt—that Chinese shadow play.

Does anyone still say a prayer
Before going to bed?

White sleeplessness.
No one knows its weight.

WHAT THE WHITE HAD TO SAY

*For how could anything white be distinct
from or divided from whiteness?*

Meister Eckhart

Because I am the bullet
That has gone through everyone already,
I thought of you long before you thought of me.
Each one of you still keeps a blood-stained handkerchief
In which to swaddle me, but it stays empty
And even the wind won't remain in it long.
Cleverly you've invented name after name for me,
Mixed the riddles, garbled the proverbs,
Shook your loaded dice in a tin cup,
But I do not answer back even to your curses,
For I am nearer to you than your breath.
One sun shines on us both through a crack in the roof.
A spoon brings me through the window at dawn.
A plate shows me off to the four walls
While with my tail I swing at the flies.
But there's no tail and the flies are your thoughts.
Steadily, patiently I lift your arms.
I arrange them in the posture of someone drowning,
And yet the sea in which you are sinking,
And even this night above it, is myself.

Because I am the bullet
That has baptized each one of your senses,
Poems are made of our lusty wedding nights,
The joy of words as they are written.
The ear that got up at four in the morning
To hear the grass grow inside a word.
Still, the most beautiful riddle has no answer.
I am the emptiness that tucks you in like a mockingbird's
    nest,
The fingernail that scratched on your sleep's blackboard.
Take a letter: From cloud to onion.
Say: There was never any real choice.
One gaunt shadowy mother wiped our asses,
The same old orphanage taught us loneliness.
Street-organ full of blue notes,
I am the monkey dancing to your grinding—
And still you are afraid—and so,
It's as if we had not budged from the beginning.
Time slopes. We are falling head over heels
At the speed of night. That milk tooth
You left under the pillow, it's grinning.

1970-1980

Charon's
Cosmology

THE PARTIAL EXPLANATION

Seems like a long time
Since the waiter took my order.
Grimy little luncheonette,
The snow falling outside.

Seems like it has grown darker
Since I last heard the kitchen door
Behind my back
Since I last noticed
Anyone pass on the street.

A glass of ice water
Keeps me company
At this table I chose myself
Upon entering.

And a longing,
Incredible longing
To eavesdrop
On the conversation
Of cooks.

THE LESSON

It occurs to me now
that all these years
I have been
the idiot pupil
of a practical joker.

Diligently
and with foolish reverence
I wrote down
what I took to be
his wise pronouncements
concerning
my life on earth.
Like a parrot
I rattled off the dates
of wars and revolutions.
I rejoiced
at the death of my tormentors
I even became convinced
that their number
was diminishing.

It seemed to me
that gradually
my teacher was revealing to me
a pattern,
that what I was being told
was an intricate plot
of a picaresque novel
in installments,
the last pages of which
would be given over
entirely
to lyrical evocations
of nature.

Unfortunately,
with time,
I began to detect in myself
an inability
to forget even
the most trivial detail.
I lingered more and more
over the beginnings:
The haircut of a soldier
who was urinating
against our fence;
shadows of trees on the ceiling,
the day
my mother and I
had nothing to eat . . .

Somehow,
I couldn't get past
that prison train
that kept waking me up
every night.
I couldn't get that whistle
that rumble
out of my head . . .

In this classroom
austerely furnished
by my insomnia,
at the desk consisting
of my two knees,
for the first time
in this long and terrifying
apprenticeship,
I burst out laughing.
Forgive me, all of you!
At the memory of my uncle
charging a barricade
with a homemade bomb,
I burst out laughing.

A LANDSCAPE
WITH CRUTCHES

So many crutches. Now even the daylight
Needs one, even the smoke
As it goes up. And the shacks—
One per customer—they move off
In a single file with difficulty,

I said, with a hell of an effort . . .
And the trees behind them about to stumble,
And the ants on their toy-crutches,
And the wind on its ghost-crutch.

I can't get any peace around here:
The bread on its artificial limbs,
A headless doll in a wheelchair,
And my mother, mind you, using
Two knives for crutches as she squats to pee.

THE VARIANT

A police dog eating grass
On a coroner's leash
Along the perimeter
Of barbed wire.

His impeccable table manners
And the evening's capacity
For lofty detachment
From the extraordinary event.

The grass like a prophet's beard,
Thoughtful and greying. Chill
Of late autumn in the air.
Distant guard-towers with searchlights
Following us all
With malice, regret,
And also absent-mindedly.

The proverbial dry blades
Sticking in the throat.

Obviously, what the poor mutt needs
Is a mean old stepmother
To tap him on the back
Quickly
Not caring to hold on.

THE SUMMONS

The robes of the judges are magnificent
When they make their entrance among the assembled.
The one with the head of a lamb will be mine,
The one with a throat of a lamb recently slit

Who rests his cheekbone against my summons.
The one already half-salted, half-roasted
Whose eyes and mouth are full of rosemary,
Who presides today in this old courtroom,

This huge ruin with its roof badly gutted
So one can see the sky. Dark clouds and white snowflakes
Whirling in the vast empty space
Over which we address each other,

Over which we proclaim our identical innocence,
These silent snowflakes as our witnesses,
And the old cleaning women who sweep them,
Knowing each flake by its suffering and name.

POEM

My father writes all day, all night:
Writes while he sleeps, writes in his coffin.
It's nice and quiet in our house.
You can see the specks of dust in the sunlight.

I look at times over his shoulders
At all that whiteness. The snow is falling,
As you'd expect. A drop of ink
Gets buried easily, like a footprint.

I, too, would get lost but there's his shadow
On the wall, like a perched owl.
There's the sound of his pen
And the bottle on the table sunk in thought.

When the bottle empties
His great dark hand
Bigger than the earth
Feels for the moon's spigot.

NURSERY RHYME

The little pig goes to market.
Historical necessity. I like to recite
While you prefer to write on the blackboard.
Leap frog and marbles.

Their heads are big and their noses are short.
Lovely afternoon. The firing squad.
A street maimed so it can go on begging.
Eternal recurrence and its trash heap.

Follow your calling, we follow ours.
The soldier's hand is gentle. The green meadow.
People who snore have happy dreams.
Our father in heaven loves us all.

A pig with gold teeth, says the barber.
Banks of a river lined with willows.
Now someone's kicking him to hurry up.
Rope, give a drink of milk to the rope.

I need another cigarette quickly.
An execution. The old wedding photograph.
I see a blur, a speck, meager, receding,
Our lives trailing in its wake.

HELP WANTED

They ask for a knife
I come running
They need a lamb
I introduce myself as the lamb

A thousand sincere apologies
It seems they require some rat-poison
They require a shepherd
For their flock of black widows

Luckily I've brought my bloody
Letters of recommendation
I've brought my death certificate
Signed and notarized

But they've changed their minds again
Now they want a song-bird a bit of springtime
They want a woman
To soap and kiss their balls

It's one of my many talents
(I assure them)
Chirping and whistling like an aviary
Spreading the cheeks of my ass

ANIMAL ACTS

A bear who eats with a silver spoon.
Two apes adept at grave-digging.
Rats who do calculus.
A police dog who copulates with a woman,
Who takes undertaker's measurements.

A bedbug who suffers, who has doubts
About his existence. The miraculous
Laughing dove. A thousand-year-old turtle
Playing billiards. A chicken who
Cuts his own throat, who bleeds.

The trainer with his sugar-cubes,
With his chair and whip. The evenings
When they all huddle in a cage,
Smoking cheap cigars, lazily
Marking the cards in the new deck.

CHARON'S COSMOLOGY

With only his dim lantern
To tell him where he is
And every time a mountain
Of fresh corpses to load up

Take them to the other side
Where there are plenty more
I'd say by now he must be confused
As to which side is which

I'd say it doesn't matter
No one complains he's got
Their pockets to go through
In one a crust of bread in another a sausage

Once in a long while a mirror
Or a book which he throws
Overboard into the dark river
Swift and cold and deep

HAPPY END

And then they pressed the melon
And heard it crack
And then they ate enough to burst
And then the bird sung oh so sweetly
While they sat scratching without malice
Good I said for just then
The cripples started dancing on the table
That night I met a kind of angel
Do you have a match she said
As I was unzipping her dress
Already there were plenty of them
Who had ascended to the ceiling
Lovers they were called and they held
Roses between their teeth while the Spring
Went on outside the wide open windows
And even a stick used in childbeating
Blossomed by the little crooked road
My hunch told me to follow

THE BALLAD OF THE WHEEL

so that's what it's like to be a wheel
so that's what it's like to be tied to one of its spokes
while the rim screeches while the hub grinds
so that's what it's like to have the earth and heaven
    confused
to speak of the stars on the road
of stones churning in the icy sky
to suffer as the wheel suffers
to bear its unimaginable weight

if only it were a honing wheel
I would have its sparks to see by
if only it were a mill stone
I would have bread to keep my mouth busy
if only it were a roulette wheel
my left eye would watch its right dance in it

so that's what it's like
to be chained to the wounded rib of a wheel
to move as the hearse moves
to move as the lumber truck moves
down the mountains at night

       ◆

what do you think my love
while the wheel turns

I think of the horse out in front
how the snowflakes are caught in his mane
how he shakes his beautiful blindfolded head
I think how in the springtime
two birds are pulling us along as they fly
how one bird is a crow

and the other a swallow
I think how in the summertime
there's no one out there
except the clouds in the blue sky
except the dusk in the blue sky
I think how in autumn
there's a man harnessed out there
a bearded man with the bit stuck in his mouth
a hunchback with a blanket over his shoulders
hauling the wheel
heavy as the earth

♦

don't you hear I say don't you hear
the wheel talk as it turns

I have the impression that it's hugging me closer
that it has maternal instincts
that it's telling me a bedtime story
that it knows the way home
that I grit my teeth just like my father

I have the impression
that it whispers to me
how all I have to do
to stop its turning
is to hold my breath

A WALL

That's the only image
That turns up.

A wall all by itself,
Poorly lit, beckoning,
But no sense of the room,
Not even a hint
Of why it is I remember
So little and so clearly:

The fly I was watching,
The details of its wings
Glowing like turquoise.
Its feet, to my amusement
Following a minute crack—
An eternity
Around that simple event.

And nothing else; and nowhere
To go back to;
And no one else
As far as I know to verify.

DESCRIPTION

That which brings it
about. The cause.

The sweet old temptation
to find an equivalent

for the ineffable:
This street, this gray day

breaking. So many things
for which to find a name.

Standing here, partaking
of that necessity.

◆

Among all the sights
that offer themselves,

where to begin?
The visible, the invisible—

the many shapes pain assumes?
This old woman, for instance,

with a lame child,
leading her by the hand,

the way they suffer
to take every little step.

◆

A street which always
somehow resembles me.

Gray day and I
the source of its grayness.

A corner where
a part of myself

keeps an appointment
with another part of myself.

This small world.
This dumb show.

◆

The two of them
all hunched up,

hand in hand,
afraid to cross the street

on some age-old errand
to a store, a hospital

where the grim doctor
won't use any anaesthetic

when he takes bread
out of their mouths.

THE TERMS

A child crying in the night
Across the street
In one of the many dark windows.
That, too, to get used to,
Make part of your life.
Like this book of astronomy
Which you open with equal apprehension
By the light of table lamp,
And your bird-like shadow on the wall.
A sleepless witness at the base
Of this expanding immensity,
Simultaneous in this moment
With all of its empty spaces,
Listening to a child crying in the night
With a hope,
It will go on crying a little longer.

ERASER

A summons because the marvelous prey is fleeing
Something to rub out the woods
From the blackboard sound of wind and rain
A device to recover a state of pure expectancy

Only the rubbings only the endless patience
As the clearing appears the clearing which is there
Without my even having to look
The domain of the marvelous prey

This emptiness which gets larger and larger
As the eraser works and wears out
As my mother shakes her apron full of little erasers
For me to peck like breadcrumbs

TRAVELLING
SLAUGHTERHOUSE

Dürer, I like that horse of yours.
I spent my childhood hidden in his guts.
The knight looks like my father
The day he came out of prison.

Maria, the redheaded girl goes by
Without giving us a nod. The knight says,
I get up at night to see if the table is still a table.
He says, when I close my eyes everything is
    so damn pretty.

We are dawdling in our old backalley.
I see a dog, a goat, but no death.
It must be one of those bleak breezy days in late autumn.
The horse uses his tail to hold up his pants.

Maria naked in front of a mirror eating an apple.
He says, I love the hair on the nipple to be blonde.
He says, we are a travelling slaughterhouse.
Ah the poor horse, he lets me eat his heart out!

EYES FASTENED
WITH PINS

How much death works,
No one knows what a long
Day he puts in. The little
Wife always alone
Ironing death's laundry.
The beautiful daughters
Setting death's supper table.
The neighbors playing
Pinochle in the backyard
Or just sitting on the steps
Drinking beer. Death,
Meanwhile, in a strange
Part of town looking for
Someone with a bad cough,
But the address somehow wrong,
Even death can't figure it out
Among all the locked doors . . .
And the rain beginning to fall.
Long windy night ahead.
Death with not even a newspaper
To cover his head, not even
A dime to call the one pining away,
Undressing slowly, sleepily,
And stretching naked
On death's side of the bed.

TREES AT NIGHT

Putting out the light
To hear them better

◆

To tell the leaves
Of an ash tree
Apart from those
Of a white birch.

◆

They would both
Come closer,
They would both whisk me away

◆

Images of birds
Fleeing from a fire,
Images of a lifeboat
Caught in the storm.

◆

The sound of those
Who sleep without dreams.

◆

Being taken hold of
By them.
Being actively taken hold of,
Being carried off
In throes.

♦

At times also like the tap
Of a moth
On a windowscreen.

♦

A flurry of thoughts.
Sediments
On the bottom of night's ink,
Seething, subsiding.

♦

Branches bending
To the boundaries
Of the inaudible.

♦

A prolonged hush
That reminds me
To lock the doors.

♦

Clarity.
The mast of my spine, for instance,
To which death attaches
A fluttering handkerchief.

♦

And the wind makes
A big deal out of it.

EUCLID AVENUE

All my dark thoughts
laid out
in a straight line.

An abstract street
on which an equally abstract intelligence
forever advances, doubting
the sound of its own footsteps.

◆

Interminable cortege.
Language
as old as rain.
Fortune-teller's spiel

from where it has its beginning,
its kennel and bone,
the scent of a stick
I used to retrieve.

◆

A sort of darkness without the woods,
crow-light but without the crow,
Hotel Splendide
all locked up for the night.

And out there,
in sight of some ultimate bakery
the street-light
of my insomnia.

♦

A place
known as infinity
toward which that old self
advances.

The poor son of poor parents
who aspires to please
at such a late hour.

The magical coins
in his pocket
occupying all his thoughts.

A place known
as infinity,
its screendoor screeching,
endlessly screeching.

THE PRISONER

He is thinking of us.
These leaves, their lazy rustle
That made us sleepy after lunch
So we had to lie down.

He considers my hand on her breast,
Her closed eyelids, her moist lips
Against my forehead, and the shadows of trees
Hovering on the ceiling.

It's been so long. He has trouble
Deciding what else is there.
And all along the suspicion
That we do not exist.

A DAY MARKED WITH
A SMALL WHITE STONE

The kindest of traps
Despite its immaculate steel,
And its powerful spring.
The bait, too, which one inhales
As if it were a scent of mint
The breeze is carrying.

The languorous, lazy chewing
On the caught leg
Gnawed down to the bone.
Pain joining the silence
Of trees and white clouds,

In a ring
Of magnanimous coyotes,
In a ring of
Dreamy, once-in-a-lifetime
Something or other.

POSITION WITHOUT
A MAGNITUDE

As when someone
You haven't noticed before
Gets up in an empty theater
And projects his shadow
Among the fabulous horsemen
On the screen

And you shudder
As you realize it's only you
On your way
To the blinding sunlight
Of the street.

Classic
Ballroom
Dances

PRIMER

This kid got so dirty
Playing in the ashes

When they called him home,
When they yelled his name over the ashes,

It was a lump of ashes
That answered.

Little lump of ashes, they said,
Here's another lump of ashes for dinner,

To make you sleepy,
And make you grow strong.

SCHOOL FOR
DARK THOUGHTS

At daybreak,
Little one,
I can feel the immense weight
Of the books you carry.

Anonymous one,
I can hardly make you out
In that large crowd
On the frozen playground.

Simple one,
There are rulers and sponges
Along the whitewashed walls
Of the empty classroom.

There are windows
And blackboards,
One can only see through
With eyes closed.

EMPIRE OF DREAMS

On the first page of my dreambook
It's always evening
In an occupied country.
Hour before the curfew.
A small provincial city.
The houses all dark.
The store-fronts gutted.

I am on a street corner
Where I shouldn't be.
Alone and coatless
I have gone out to look
For a black dog who answers to my whistle.
I have a kind of halloween mask
Which I am afraid to put on.

PRODIGY

I grew up bent over
a chessboard.

I loved the word *endgame*.

All my cousins looked worried.

It was a small house
near a Roman graveyard.
Planes and tanks
shook its windowpanes.

A retired professor of astronomy
taught me how to play.

That must have been in 1944.

In the set we were using,
the paint had almost chipped off
the black pieces.

The white King was missing
and had to be substituted for.

I'm told but do not believe
that that summer I witnessed
men hung from telephone poles.

I remember my mother
blindfolding me a lot.

She had a way of tucking my head
suddenly under her overcoat.

In chess, too, the professor told me,
the masters play blindfolded,
the great ones on several boards
at the same time.

BABY PICTURES OF
FAMOUS DICTATORS

The epoch of a streetcar drawn by horses;
The organ-grinder and his monkey.
Women with parasols. Little kids in rowboats
Photographed against a cardboard backdrop depicting an
idyllic sunset
At the fairgrounds where they all went to see
The two-headed calf, the bearded
Fat lady who dances the dance of seven veils.

And the great famine raging through India . . .
Fortune-telling white rats pulling a card out of shoebox
While Edison worries over the lightbulb,
And the first model of the sewing machine
Is delivered in a pushcart
To a modest white-fenced home in the suburbs,

Where there are always a couple of infants
Posing for the camera in their sailors' suits,
Out there in the garden overgrown with shrubs.
Lovable little mugs smiling faintly toward
The new century. Innocent. Why not?
All of them like ragdolls of the period
With those chubby porcelain heads
That shut their long eyelashes as you lay them down.

In a kind of perpetual summer twilight . . .
One can even make out the shadow of the tripod and the black
    hood
That must have been quivering in the breeze.
One assumes that they all stayed up late squinting at the stars,
And were carried off to bed by their mothers and big sisters,
While the dogs remained behind:
Pedigreed bitches pregnant with bloodhounds.

WHISPERS
IN THE NEXT ROOM

The hospital barber, for instance,
Who shaves the stroke victims,
Shaves lunatics in strait-jackets,
Doesn't even provide a mirror,

Is a widower, has a dog waiting
At home, a canary from a dimestore . . .
Eats beans cold from a can,
Then scrapes the bottom with his spoon . . .

Says: No one has seen me today,
Oh Lord, as I too have seen
No one, not even myself,
Bent as I was, intently, over the razor.

SHIRT

To get into it
As it lies
Crumpled on the floor
Without disturbing a single crease

Respectful
Of the way I threw it down
Last night
The way it happened to land

Almost managing
The impossible contortions
Doubling back now
Through a knotted sleeve

GREAT INFIRMITIES

Everyone has only one leg.
So difficult to get around,
So difficult to climb the stairs
Without a cane or a crutch to our name.

And only one arm. Impossible contortions
Just to embrace the one you love,
To cut the bread on the table,
To put a coat on in a hurry.

I should mention that we are almost blind,
And a little deaf in both ears.
Perilous to be on the street
Among the congregations of the afflicted.

With only a few steps committed to memory,
Meekly we let ourselves be diverted
In the endless twilight—
Blind seeing-eye dogs on our leashes.

An immense stillness everywhere
With the trees always bare,
The raindrops coming down only halfway,
Coming so close and giving up.

THE HEALER

In a rundown tenement
Under the superhighway,
A healer lives
Who doesn't believe in his power.

An old man with a fat gut,
Hands of a little girl
Which he manicures himself,
Carefully, between visits.

In his hallway there are
Many wheelchairs, on the stairs
The long howl of the idiot
Led on his mother's leash.

NAVIGATOR

I summoned Christopher Columbus.
At the hour of the wolf,
He came out of the gloom
Looking a little like my father.

On this particular voyage
He discovered nothing.
The ocean I gave him had no end,
And the ship—an open suitcase.

He was thoroughly lost. I had forgotten to provide
    the stars.
Sitting in the dark with a bottle in his hand.
He sang a song from his childhood.

In the song the day was breaking.
A barefoot girl
Stepped over the wet grass
To pick a sprig of mint.

And then nothing—
Only the wind rushing off with a screech
As if it just remembered
Where it's going, where it's been.

A SUITCASE STRAPPED
WITH A ROPE

For Jim

They made themselves so tiny
They could all fit in one suitcase.
The suitcase they kept under the bed,
And the bed near the open window.

They huddled there in the dark
While their mother called out their names
To make sure no one was missing.
Her voice made them warm, made them sleepy.

He wanted to go out and play.
He even asked for permission.
They told him to be very quiet.
Just then the suitcase was moving.

Soon the border guards were going
To open it and inspect it,
Unless, of course, it was a burglar
And he knew another way to go.

BEGOTTEN OF THE SPLEEN

The Virgin Mother walked barefoot
Among the land mines.
She carried an old man in her arms
Like a howling babe.

The earth was an old people's home.
Judas was the night nurse,
Emptying bedpans into the river Jordan,
Tying people on a dog chain.

The old man had two stumps for legs.
St. Peter came pushing a cart
Loaded with flying carpets.
They were not flying carpets.

They were piles of bloody diapers.
The Magi stood around
Cleaning their nails with bayonets.
The old man gave little Mary Magdalene

A broken piece of a mirror.
She hid in the church outhouse.
When she got thirsty she licked
The steam off the glass.

That leaves Joseph. Poor Joseph,
Standing naked in the snow.
He only had a rat
To load his suitcases on.

The rat wouldn't run into its hole.
Even when the lights came on—
And the lights came on:
The floodlights in the guard towers.

TOY FACTORY

My mother works here,
And so does my father.

It's the night shift.
At the assembly line.
They wind toys up
To inspect their springs.

The seven toy members
Of the firing squad
Point their rifles,
And lower them quickly.

The one being shot at
Falls and gets up,
Falls and gets up.
His blindfold is just painted on.

The toy gravediggers
Don't work so well.
Their spades are heavy,
Their spades are much too heavy.

Perhaps that's how
It's supposed to be?

THE LITTLE TEAR-GLAND
THAT SAYS

Then there was Johann,
the carrousel horse—
except he wasn't really a carrousel horse.

He grew up in "the naive realism of the Wolffian school
which without close scrutiny regards
logical necessity and reality as identical."

On Sundays, his parents took him
to the undertaker's for sugar.
"All these people flying in their dreams,"
he thought.

Standing before the Great Dark Night of History,
a picture of innocence
held together by his mother's safety pins,
frisky, wagging his tail.

Cool reflection soon showed
there were openings among the signatories
        of death certificates...
with those high leather boots that squeak.

On his entrance exam he wrote:
"The act of torture consists of various strategies
meant to increase the imagination
of the *homo sapiens.*"

And then...The Viennese waltz.

THE STREAM

for Russ Banks

The ear threading
the eye

all night long
the ear
on a long errand
for the eye

through the thickening
pine
white birch
over no man's land

pebbles
is it
compact in their anonymity
their gravity

accidents of location
abstract necessity

water
which takes such pains
to convince me
it is flowing

◆

Summoning me
to be
two places at once

to drift
the length
of its chill
its ache

hand white
at the knuckles

live bait
the old hide and seek
in and out
of the swirl

luminous verb
carnivorous verb
innocent as sand
under its blows

♦

An insomnia as big
as the stars'

always
on the brink —
as it were
of some deeper utterance

some harsher
reckoning

at daybreak

lightly
oh so lightly
when she brushes
against me

and the hems of her long skirt
go trailing

a bit longer

♦

Nothing
that comes to nothing
for company

comes the way a hurt
the way a thought
comes

comes and keeps coming

all night meditating
on what she asks of me
when she doesn't

when I hear myself say
she doesn't

THE WAY IT IS

If a cuckoo comes into the village
Of cuckoos to cuckoo and it's Monday,
And all the cuckoos should be out working,
But instead there's no one around,

No one at home, no one in the fields
Overgrown with weeds...
O then, the cuckoo who came to the village
Of cuckoos to cuckoo must cuckoo alone.

FURNITURE MOVER

Ah the great
  the venerable
whoever he is

  ahead of me
huge load
  terrific backache

  wherever
a chair's waiting
  meadow
sky
  beckoning

he is the one
  that's been
there
  without instructions
and for no wages

  a huge load
on his back
  and under his arm
thus
  always

  all in place
perfect
  just as it was
sweet home

at the address
I never even dreamed of
the address
I'm already changing

in a hurry
to overtake him
to arrive
not ahead

but just as
he sets down
the table
the thousand-year-old
bread crumbs

I used to
claim
I was part
of his load

high up there
roped safely
with the junk
the eviction notices

I used to
prophesy
he'll stumble
by and by

No luck—
oh
Mr. Furniture Mover
on my knees

let me come
for once
early
to where it's vacant

you still
on the stairs
wheezing
between floors

and me behind the door
in the gloom
I think I would
let you do

what you must

ELEGY

Note
as it gets darker
   that little
can be ascertained
of the particulars
   and of their true
magnitudes

   note
the increasing
   unreliability
of vision
though one thing may appear
   more or less
familiar
   than another

   disengaged
from reference
as they are
   in the deepening
gloom

   nothing to do
but sit
   and abide
depending on memory
to provide

the vague outline
the theory
of where we are
tonight

and why
we can see
so little
of each other
and soon
will be
even less
able

in this starless
summer night
windy and cold

at the table
brought out
hours ago
under a huge ash tree

two chairs
two ambiguous figures
  each only relying
on the other
to remain faithful
  now
that one can leave
  without the other one
  knowing

  this late
in what only recently was
  a garden
a festive occasion
  elaborately planned
for two lovers

  in the open air
at the end
  of a dead-end
road
  rarely traveled

  o love

NOTE
SLIPPED UNDER A DOOR

I saw a high window struck blind
By the late afternoon sunlight.

I saw a towel
With many dark fingerprints
Hanging in the kitchen.

I saw an old apple tree,
A shawl of wind over its shoulders,
Inch its lonely way
Toward the barren hills.

I saw an unmade bed
And felt the cold of its sheets.

I saw a fly soaked in pitch
Of the coming night
Watching me because it couldn't get out.

I saw stones that had come
From a great purple distance
Huddle around the front door.

DECEMBER TREES

Dark woods, I give myself entirely over
To your master craftsmen. In a clearing
They sized me up and then took their time.
Quiet folk, tall, emaciated,

For such is the season. Obligingly
With hands raised high, I stood like a horse
Being shod in a blacksmith's shop.
Smoke of a late December sunlight all around us.

Great bellows of approaching dusk,
As the birches put on their aprons
And reached among their branches for irons,
The black ones with night frost on.

GROCERY

Figure or figures unknown
Keep a store
Keep it open
Nights and all day Sunday

Half of what they sell
Will kill you
The other half
Makes you go back for more

Too cheap to turn on the lights
Hard to tell what it is
They've got on the counter
What it is you're paying for

All the rigors
All the solemnities
Of a brass scale imperceptibly quivering
In the early winter dusk

One of its pans
For their innards
The other one for yours—
And yours heavier

CLASSIC BALLROOM DANCES

Grandmothers who wring the necks
Of chickens; old nuns
With names like Theresa, Marianne,
Who pull schoolboys by the ear;

The intricate steps of pickpockets
Working the crowd of the curious
At the scene of an accident; the slow shuffle
Of the evangelist with a sandwich-board;

The hesitation of the early morning customer
Peeking through the window-grille
Of a pawnshop; the weave of a little kid
Who is walking to school with eyes closed;

And the ancient lovers, cheek to cheek,
On the dancefloor of the Union Hall,
Where they also hold charity raffles
On rainy Monday nights of an eternal November.

HARSH CLIMATE

The brain itself in its skull
Is very cold,
According to
Albertus Magnus.

Something like a stretch of tundra
On the scale of the universe.
Galactic wind.
Lofty icebergs in the distance.

Polar night.
A large ocean liner caught in the ice.
A few lights still burning on the deck.
Silence and fierce cold.

PEACEFUL KINGDOM

The bird who watches me
sleeping
from the branch of an apple tree
in bloom.

A black bird
for whom a strange man
gathers rocks
in the ruts of the road.

♦

And among the willow trees:
water
before water made up its mind
to be water.

My sister says if I drink
of that water I will die . . .
That's why the heart beats:
to waken the water.

BEDTIME STORY

When a tree falls in a forest
And there's no one around
To hear the sound, the poor owls
Have to do all the thinking.

They think so hard they fall off
Their perch and are eaten by ants,
Who, as you already know, all look like
Little Black Riding Hoods.

THE TOMB OF
STÉPHANE MALLARMÉ

Beginning to know
   how the die
navigates
   how it makes
its fateful decisions
   in eternal circumstances
what it feels like
   to be held tight
between the thumb
   and the forefinger
to be hexed
   and prayed over
to wake up lucid
   at the heart of the shipwreck
a dark pilot's cabin
   of the die on the move
to have the earth and heaven
   repeatedly reversed
to have the mirror and the razor
   momentarily aligned
only to fall
   head over heels
to be set adrift
   in the middle of
nowhere

the die
worn clean
by endless conjectures
my die
perfectly illegible
white
as a milk tooth
the perfect die
rolling
picking up speed
how delightful
this new contingency
occupancy
both inside and outside
the unthinkable

the blindman's die
free of
the divinatory urge
the Number
even if it existed
the death-defying
somersault
beating the supreme odds
two by two
along for the ride
only
the roller-coaster
endlessly changing directions
and mind
in a state of blessed
uncertainty

cast
   on the great improbable
table
   among the ghostly salt-cellars
bones
   breadcrumbs that say
there goes:
   Cerberus's new toy
Death's great amateur
   night
the childhood of Parmenides

oh yeah

FOREST BIRDS

It! It!
That's what the unknown bird said,

and another answered,
in the same manner,

without identifying the agent:
some animal or thing.

Very cautious of them,
to be sure.

With the woods so thick and murky,
poor unknown...

A frailest twig,
and then the tip of that twig
to speak from...

It looks like it,
and it acts like it,
but who's to say?

◆

That *it*
has wish
that *it*
has a wishbone

deep, deep
in all our throats

which is why the birds
are screeching...

in the vicinity of,
in the terrifying

nearness of...

♦

The woods of the obscure,
the hidden.

The woods of the lost,
the woods of the innermost,
inwrought, indwelling

object of our desire.

A name called from
one of its giddiest branches.

Odd name proclaimed
oddly.

Harken to *it* to be sure.

♦

By eaves and leaves...

How like leave-
taking.

How like St. Francis
saying:

little brother,
little sister.

Last half-note,
half-twig.

I'm very anxious,
they're very anxious

to have it remain
like that.

Weather Forecast For Utopia & Vicinity

FIGURING

A zero burped by
Another huger zero
That says woe woe!

The whole orphanage
Came out to see.

We gave it feathers,
Wings of an angel.
We gave it the shirt off our backs.

Potato head, egg of a snowy owl,
But the forest veiled,
The Papa and Mama forest.

Wintry pallor and ire.
Wind's rabies. Pitchy heavens.

Apes with rice-powdered asses.
Monday moving its dentures.

We give it a race horse,
Windmills, an alarm clock with one hand.
Off it goes, trussed up, slaphappy.

At the other end of a zoo cage
A nurse waits for him,
Rainy days, stub of a pencil.

A zero. Write it kid!

And he writes it.
The dumb-looking one
At the blackboard.

HISTORY BOOK

A kid found its loose pages
On a busy street.
He stopped bouncing his ball
To run after them.

They fluttered in his hands
And flew off.
He could only glimpse
A few dates and a name.

At the outskirts the wind
Lost interest in them.
Some fell into the river
By the old railroad bridge

Where they drown kittens,
And the barge passes,
The one they named "Victory"
From which a cripple waves.

GRAVITY

I'd like to see it once
As it lowers
Its fat foot
On our shoulders.

O Lord! That's what the choir
Of the Baptist church says,
And the trees agree
As they bend low in observance.

Sunday evening service
Where it wants the congregation
On its knees, sighing
And kissing the floor,

And later,
Still swaying under its weight,
Like beasts of burden,
Going home over the freshly fallen snow.

NORTHERN EXPOSURE

When old women say, it smells of snow,
In a whisper barely audible
Which still rouses the sick man upstairs
So he opens his eyes wide and lets them fill

With the grayness of the remaining daylight.
When old women say, how quiet it is,
And truly today no one came to visit,
While the one they still haven't shaved

Lifts the wristwatch to his ear and listens.
In it, something small, subterranean
And awful in intent, chews rapidly.
When old women say, time to turn on the lights,

And not a single one gets up to do so,
For now there are loops and loose knots around their feet
As if someone is scribbling over them
With a piece of charcoal found in the cold stove.

WINTER NIGHT

The church is an iceberg.

It's the wind. It must be blowing tonight
Out of those galactic orchards,
Their Copernican pits and stones.

The monster created by the mad Dr. Frankenstein
Sailed for the New World,
And ended up some place like New Hampshire.

Actually, it's just a local drunk,
Knocking with a snow shovel,
Wanting to go in and warm himself.

An iceberg, the book says, is a large drifting
Piece of ice, broken off a glacier.

THE COLD

As if in a presence of an intelligence
Concentrating. I thought myself
Scrutinized and measured closely
By the sky and the earth,

And then algebraized and entered
In a notebook page blank and white,
Except for the faint blue lines
Which might have been bars,

For I kept walking and walking,
And it got darker and then there was
A flicker of a light or two
Far above and beyond my big cage.

A FALL DAY

As gray as that slumped
Figure hands deep in his
Pockets receding on the
Gravelly road lean dogs
From the trailer park on
His ass the whole soulful
Lot of them fading away
Without *adieus* fading
Because of all the fine sands
Piling up on lunar deserts
Which have a way of sifting
Down this way the late
Autumn light already grainy
Gritty like poor eyesight
Gray bedsheets gray back
Of a woman combing her
Graying hair under the dead
Clock on the wall
Because truth's gray
Naked truth looking out
Vacant-eyed on the rain-
Blurred weedchoked outskirts
Of a dying milltown
Where her ancient mother
Keeps giving that last dime
To someone wearing a hood
Of yesterday's newspapers
Outside the urine-streaked
Theater-lobby where on Saturday
Nights they've Live Wrestling
Teeth filed to razor's sharpness

Lion-roars mad-dog-bites
Backbreakers you'd hear in China
But now all of it mute cindery
Grim and earnest
Unlettered and benighted
I believe hieroglyphically

OLD COUPLE

They're waiting to be murdered,
Or evicted. Soon
They expect to have nothing to eat.
In the meantime, they sit.

A violent pain is coming, they think.
It will start in the heart
And climb into the mouth.
They'll be carried off in stretchers, howling.

Tonight they watch the window
Without exchanging a word.
It has rained, and now it looks
Like it's going to snow a little.

I see him get up to lower the shades.
If their window stays dark,
I know his hand has reached hers
Just as she was about to turn on the lights.

COLD BLUE TINGE

The pink-cheeked Jesus
Thumb-tacked above
The cold gas stove,
And the boy sitting on the pisspot
Blowing soap-bubbles
For the black kitten to catch.

Very peaceful, except
There's a faint moan
From the next room.
His mother's asking
For some more pills,
But there's no reply.
The bubbles are quiet,
And kitten is sleepy.

All his brothers and sisters
Have been drowned.
He'll have a long life, though,
Catching mice for the baker,
And the undertaker.

THE WRITINGS OF THE MYSTICS

On the counter among many
Much-used books,
The rare one you must own
Immediately, the one
That makes your heart race

As you wait for small change
With a silly grin
You'll take to the street,
And later, past the landlady
Watching you wipe your shoes,

Then, up to the rented room
Which neighbors the one
Of a nightclub waitress
Who's shaving her legs
With a door partly open,

While you turn to the first page
Which speaks of a presentiment
Of a higher existence
In things familiar and drab . . .

In a house soon to be torn down,
Suddenly hushed, and otherworldly . . .
You have to whisper your own name,
And the words of the hermit,

Since it must be long past dinner,
The one they ate quickly
Happy that your small portion
Went to the three-legged dog.

WINDOW WASHER

And again the screech of the scaffold
High up there where all our thoughts converge:
Lightheaded, hung
By a leather strap,

Twenty stories up
In the chill of late November
Wiping the grime
Off the pane, the many windows

Which have no way of opening,
Tinted windows mirroring the clouds
That are like equestrian statues,
Phantom liberators with sabers raised

Before these dark offices,
And their anonymous multitudes
Bent over this day's
Wondrously useless labor.

THE GAME

A child played being a gravedigger.

Yellow pail and plastic shovel
On the green meadow.
Night coming.
Huge clouds rolling in.

With his stooped shoulders
He looks busy in the obvious way...
Dark, damp clods of earth flying.

They ought to call him in by now:
The carrot-haired girl in the hen house;
Her sister at the salt-lick.

GALLOWS ETIQUETTE

Our sainted great-great
Grandmothers
Used to sit and knit
Under the gallows.

No one remembers what it is
They were knitting
And what happened when the ball of yarn
Rolled out of their laps
And had to be retrieved?

One pictures the hooded executioner
And his pasty-faced victim
Interrupting their grim business
To come quickly to their aid.

Confirmed pessimists
And other party-poopers
Categorically reject
Such far-fetched notions
Of gallows etiquette.

IN MIDSUMMER QUIET

Ariadne's bird,
That lone
Whip-poor-will.

Ball of twilight-thread
Unraveling furtively.
Tawny thread,
Raw, pink the thread-end.

A claw or two also
To pare, snip...
After which it sits still
For the stream to explain why it shivers

So.
        Resuming, farther on,
Intermittently,
By the barn
Where the first stars are—
In quotation marks,
As it were—O phantom

Bird!
Dreaming of my own puzzles
And mazes.

PEACEFUL TREES

in memory of M.N.

All shivers,
Dear friends.

Is it for me
You keep still?

Not a rustle
To remind me—

Quietly, the healing
Spreads—

A deep shade
Over each face.

◆

So many leaves,
And not one
Lately stirring.

So many already
Tongue-shaped,
Tip of the tongue shaped.

Oh the sweet speech of trees
In the evening breeze
Of some other summer.

Speech like sudden
Rustle of raindrops
Out of the high, pitch-blue
Heavens.

Lofty ones,
Do you shudder
When the chainsaw
Cuts one of you?

Would it soothe,
If for all you voiceless,
To high heavens
The one with the rope round his neck

Were to plead?

♦

Forgive me,

For the conjecture
I'm prone to —

Restless as I am
Before you windless,

Whispering
To the Master-Whisperers

Of their own
Early evening silences.

THE MAN

Some Power Company Employee
Whose job it is
To turn on the street-lights
In my neighborhood.

Almost night now,
And he's late, very late—
Whoever he is, must have
Other things on his mind.

For all we know,
Might be roaming these streets,
Hands in his pockets
Bumping into some of us.

Sorry and all that...
Standing here on the corner,
Smoking butts, whispering.
Stargazing a bit too.

A QUIET TALK WITH ONESELF

As spring flowers are promised by
Seed-sellers in their new catalogues,
You too were once full of promise,
Only to lapse, woefully, my friend.

Cultivated garden's perfect rows
Marshalling their bright colors —
How I hate such images —
Some rosy-cheeked Rose clipping sweetheart roses

For the ass's wreath, the dull-eyed one who ought to be rapt,
What with his easy source of sustenance:
Pulling loads of potatoes, an occasional coffin,
Or just a cart full of happy children at the fair.

It seems to me these moods are best walked off
In a straight line toward some provisional infinity,
With many head-shakes, groans too,
Under the leaves which must wonder at their own gradual
    disappearance.

But I digress. Just like that unfortunate Mr. Poe:
Compulsive ratiocination on the subject of the self
In the guise of a polar voyage without the means of retreat,
While the poor ass keeps getting whipped and rained on.

Each one of us like an ex-waiter, slightly bowed,
A linen napkin still in the crook of the arm,
Eyes on the lookout for some angelic customer to serve —
Some Daisy picking poppies instead of daisies.

Austerities

HURRICANE SEASON

Just as the world was ending
We fell in love,
Immoderately. I had a pair of

Blue pinstripe trousers
Impeccably pressed
Against misfortune;

You had a pair of silver,
Spiked-heeled shoes,
And a peekaboo blouse.

We looked swank kissing
While reflected in a pawnshop window:
Banjos and fiddles around us,

Even a gleaming tuba. I said,
Two phosphorescent minute-hands
Against the Unmeasurables,

Geniuses when it came to
Undressing each other
By slow tantalizing degrees . . .

That happened in a crepuscular hotel
That had seen better days,
Across from some sort of august state institution,

Rainblurred
With its couple of fake
Egyptian stone lions.

NOTE

A rat came on stage
During the performance
Of the school Christmas play.
Mary let out a scream
And dropped the infant
On Joseph's foot.
The three Magi remained
Frozen
In their colorful robes.
You could hear a pin drop
As the rat surveyed the manger
Momentarily
Before proceeding to the wings
Where someone hit him,
In earnest,
Once, and then twice more,
With a heavy object.

AN EVENING
WITH THE MASTER

With a tiny bird-whistle
He teases my soul out of its cage,
Makes it perch on his shoulder,
Makes it eat out of his hand:
My eyes' terror
For its dinner,
Its joys
For late night snack.

With stick and leather glove
He teaches it to copy with one of its claws
The somber writings
Of my long-suffering backbone,
The mazes to be found in my brain,
The music of my footsteps.

A soul with a falcon's hood
Bent over a school slate
Which screeches and bleeds darkly
As it lets itself be written.

SPOONS WITH REALISTIC DEAD FLIES ON THEM

I cause great many worries to my mother.
My body will run with the weeds some day.
My head will be carried by slaughterhouse ants,
The carnivorous, bloody-aproned ants.

That was never in any of your legends, O saints!
The years she spent working in a novelty store:
Joy buzzers, false beards and dead flies
To talk to between the infrequent customers.

A room rented from a minor demon.
An empty bird cage and a coffee mill for company.
A hand-operated one for her secret guardian angel
To take a turn grinding the slow hours.

Though I'm not a believer—
Neither is she, and that's why she worries,
Looks both ways crossing the street
At two gusts of nothing and nothing.

HISTORY

On a gray evening
Of a gray century,
I ate an apple
While no one was looking.

A small, sour apple
The color of woodfire
Which I first wiped
On my sleeve.

Then I stretched my legs
As far as they'd go,
Said to myself
Why not close my eyes now

Before the late
World News and Weather.

ROUGH OUTLINE

The famous torturer takes a walk
Whom does he see standing there in the snow
A pretty girl in a wedding dress
What are you doing out there all alone in the cold

You're the famous torturer much feared
I beg you to spare my love
Who is in your darkest prison cell
I wish to marry him etc.

I will not give back your bridegroom
He must be tortured tonight
By me personally
You can come along and help him lament his fate

She remained where she was
The night was cold and very long
Down by the slaughterhouse a dog-like creature howled
Then the snow started to fall again

STRICTLY BUCOLIC

for Mark and Jules

Are these mellifluous sheep,
And these the meadows made twice-melliferous by their
    bleating?
Is that the famous mechanical wind-up shepherd
Who comes with instructions and service manual?

This must be the regulation white fleece
Bleached and starched to perfection,
And we could be posing for our first communion pictures,
Except for the nasty horns.

I am beginning to think this might be
The Angelic Breeders Association's
Millennial Company Picnic (all expenses paid)
With a few large black dogs as special guests.

These dogs serve as ushers and usherettes.
They're always studying the rules,
The exigencies of proper deportment
When they're not reading Theocritus,

Or wagging their tails at the approach of
Theodora. Or is it Theodosius? Or even Theodoric?
They're theomorfic, of course. They theologize.
Theogony is their favorite. They also love theomachy.

Now they hand out the blue ribbons.
Ah, there's one for everyone!
Plus the cauldrons of stinking cabbage and boiled turnips
Which don't figure in this idyll.

CROWS

Just so that each stark,
Spiked twig,
May be even more fierce
With significance,

There are these birds
As further harbingers
Of the coming wintry reduction
To sign and enigma:

The absolutely necessary
Way in which they shook snow
Out of their wings,
And then remained, inexplicably

Thus, wings half-open,
Making two large algebraic x's
As if for emphasis,
Or in the mockery of . . .

FEBRUARY

The one who lights the wood stove
Gets up in the dark.

How cold the iron is to the hand
Groping to open the flue,
The hand that will draw back
At the roar of the wind outside.

The wood that no longer smells of the woods;
The wood that smells of rats and mice —
And the matches which are always so loud
In the glacial stillness.

By its flare you'll see her squat;
Gaunt, wide-eyed;
Her lips saying the stark headlines
Going up in flames.

INHERITANCE

This is my father's gray blanket.
He used to lie under it anonymous:
Head and face hidden, bare feet
Sticking out, their toes clenched.

On a windy November afternoon,
The house cold, even
The bright sunlight chilling,
Just as it is now —

Like a steel tape measure
Estimating the anatomy of the sleeper,
The position of the heart
Under this blanket meant for a narrow bed —

An army cot perhaps? O recruits,
Prisoners! I believe one covers one's head
Because the lights are left on
In cells throughout the night.

ROSALIA

I

An especially forlorn human specimen
Answers a marriage-ad
On a street of compulsory misfortune,
One drizzly November afternoon.
Sorrow waiting with her doilies
In a dining room with a spider-legged chandelier
Which the subway rattles from time to time.
A cup of herb tea with a bride's eyelash
Floating in it.
Homemade cakes the size and color of
A little finger caught in the door.
There's also her grandfather's saber on the wall,
And the story of how the Angel of Death
Snatched her purse
On the way home from the evening Mass.

II

She saw the Archangel Michael, too.
(That she told no one.)
She cooked dinner for her blind old mother,
Fed her with a baby spoon.
In a small, shabby office,
She entered figures in a crook's ledger,
Sharpened pencils with a razor blade.
Then she thought of Mr. O'Reilly.
Like a lone customer waiting in a barbershop
On a street of palatial funeral parlors,
A bridegroom with the eyes of someone

Who has been peeling onions,
But that can't be
Since he's in this oldtime barbershop
Empty but for the mirrors.

III

Rosalia and her mother moved away
But no one knows where and why.
They directed me to the Italian bakery.
My cakes, said the baker with the glass eye,
Are like cheeks and dimples on an old fashioned china
    doll.
Next, I stopped at the undertaker's.
We import our pillows and tassels from Arabia.
We also sell postcards of the next life —
And already, I was talking to some tarot-readers,
Madame Olga and Madame Esmeralda in spiked heels
Outside a storefront church on a windy night.
Images of Saints favored by fugitives from justice.
O trombones and tambourines!
White snowflakes falling for Rosalia Rissi
But as many lampblack ones!

PIETY

A plain black cotton dress
On a wire hanger
In a closet otherwise empty,
Its door ajar to the light.

If you open your eyes,
You'll note it sways ever so slightly,
It shudders in the draft
Of undetermined origin.

Or is it your own breath?
Reaching that far
Despite the miles of frozen
Stubble, stone, earth.

If you close your eyes,
There's even a tiny rip
On the level of thighs,
The curlicue of blackest thread.

AUSTERITIES

From the heel
Of a half loaf
Of black bread,
They made a child's head.

Child, they said,
We've nothing for eyes,
Nothing to spare for ears
And nose.

Just a knife
To make a slit
Where your mouth
Ought to be.

You can grin,
You can eat,
Spit the crumbs
Into our faces.

THUS

Blue devils'
Bluest
Offspring—
My wife.

I said,
Pascal's own
Prize abyssologist
In marriage.

On her knees
Still scrubbing
The marble stairs
Of a Russian countess.

Once long ago in Paris
Gathering the butts
Outside the fashionable cafes
For her unemployed father.

Or in the New World
Naked before the grim
Doctor and nurse
A murmur in the heart.

Nevertheless, poking
The spit-moistened
End of a black thread
At the unblinking needle's eye,

Twelve hours a day.
A sublime seamstress,
An occupation hard on the backbone
And the eyesight.

On dark winter Sundays
Difficult to squint out
The letters and foreign words
In the night school textbook.

All the carefully dog-eared,
Underlined passages
About lynchings, tar-featherings,
Witch-burnings—

Next to a cup of black coffee—
The kind storefront gypsies make
When they sit staring at the rain,
Their lips just barely moving.

SHAVING AT NIGHT

The profile of a man who waits
To be arrested at dawn.
If not this night, then
The next, the very next.

The small suitcases packed,
The wife and children long sent away,
He sits fully dressed
With the ashtray, the kitchen clock,

Thinking, maybe he should shave?
His face in the bathroom mirror
Lit by a dim bulb, one eye shut—
The face he won't look at closely—

Not yet anyway, while
There's still the upper-lip to examine,
The trembling chin, the throat
With its large adam's apple.

EAST EUROPEAN COOKING

While Marquis De Sade had himself buggered—
O just around the time the Turks
Were roasting my ancestors on spits,
Goethe wrote "The Sorrows of Young Werther."

It was chilly, raw, down-in-the-mouth
We were slurping bean soup thick with smoked sausage,
On 2nd Avenue, where years before I saw an old horse
Pull a wagon piled up high with flophouse mattresses.

Anyway, as I was telling my uncle Boris,
With my mouth full of pig's feet and wine:
"While they were holding hands and sighing under
     parasols,
We were being hung by our tongues."

"I make no distinction between scum,"
He said, and he meant everybody,
Us and them: A breed of murderers' helpers,
Evil-smelling torturers' apprentices.

Which called for another bottle of Hungarian wine,
And some dumplings stuffed with prunes
Which we devoured in silence
While the Turks went on beating their cymbals and drums.

Luckily we had this Transylvanian waiter,
A defrocked priest, ex-dancing school instructor,
Regarding whose excellence we were in complete
     agreement
Since he didn't forget the toothpicks with our bill.

THE CHILDHOOD OF PARMENIDES

for Elektra Haviaris

For asking, why is there something
Rather than nothing?
The schoolmaster sends the little punk
To see the Principal.

Unfortunately, they haven't got one yet.
There's only King Minos and his labyrinth,
And of course, Philemon, who's about to die laughing
At the sight of an ass eating figs.

DRAWING THE TRIANGLE

I reserve the triangle
For the wee hours,
The chigger-sized hours.

I like how it starts out
And never gets there.
I like how it starts out.

In the meantime, the bedroom window
Reflecting the owlish aspect
Of the face and the interior.

One hopes for tangents
Surreptitiously in attendance
Despite the rigors of the absolute.

INTERLUDE

A worm
In an otherwise
Red apple
Said: I am.

It happened on a chipped
China plate,
At a table
With twelve empty chairs.

The rightful owner
Of the apple
Had gone into the kitchen
To get a knife.

She was an old woman
Who forgot things easily.
Dear me,
She whispered.

MY WEARINESS OF EPIC
PROPORTIONS

I like it when
Achilles
Gets killed
And even his buddy Patroclus—
And that hothead Hector—
And the whole Greek and Trojan
Jeunesse doree
Is more or less
Expertly slaughtered
So there's finally
Peace and quiet
(The gods having momentarily
Shut up)
One can hear
A bird sing
And a daughter ask her mother
Whether she can go to the well
And of course she can
By that lovely little path
That winds through
The olive orchard

MADONNAS TOUCHED UP
WITH A GOATEE

Most ancient Metaphysics, (poor Metaphysics!)
All decked up in imitation jewelry.
We went for a stroll, arm in arm, smooching in public
Despite the difference in ages.

It's still the 19th century, she whispered.
We were in a knife-fighting neighborhood
Among some rundown relics of the Industrial Revolution.
Just a little further, she assured me,
In the back of a certain candy store only she knew about,
The customers were engrossed in the *Phenomenology of
the Spirit.*

It's long past midnight, my dove, my angel!
We'd better be careful, I thought.
There were young hoods on street corners
With crosses and iron studs on their leather jackets.
They all looked like they'd read Darwin and that madman
    Pavlov,
And were about to ask us for a light.

RURAL DELIVERY

I never thought we'd end up
Living this far north, love.
Cold blue heaven over our heads,
Quarter moon like chalk on a slate.

This week it's the art of subtraction
And further erasure that we study.
O the many blanks to ponder
Before the night overtakes us once more
On this lonely stretch of road
Unplowed since this morning;
Mittens raised against the sudden
Blinding gust of wind and snow,
But the mailbox empty. I had to stick
My bare hand all the way in
To make sure this is where we live.

The wonder of it! We retraced our steps
Homeward lit by the same fuel
As the snow glinting in the gloom
Of the early nightfall.

OLD MOUNTAIN ROAD

for Goody and Maida Smith

In the dusk of the evening
When the goats come,
Two pale ones nodding as they pass,
Unattended, taking their time
To graze by the curve,
Its sharpness indicated by a broken arrow,
In the last bit of daylight,

I saw a blonde little girl step
Out of nowhere, and bow to them, stiffly,
As one does at the conclusion of a school play,
And disappear, pinafore and all,
In the bushes, so that I sat
On my porch, dumbfounded . . .

The goats' intermittent tinkle
Growing fainter and fainter,
And then hushing, as if on cue,
For the whippoorwill to take over,
Briefly, in the giant maple.

Child! I thought of calling out,
Knowing myself a born doubter.

THE GREAT HORNED OWL

One morning the Grand Seigneur
Is so good as to appear.
He sits in a scrawny little tree
In my backyard.

When I say his name aloud,
He turns his head
And looks at me
In utter disbelief.

I show him my belt,
How I had to
Tighten it lately
To the final hole.

He ruffles his feathers,
Studies the empty woodshed,
The old red Chevy on blocks.
Alas! He's got to be going.

AUTUMN AIR

Many years ago in China
They studied the feasibility
Of dispelling hunger
By swallowing a lot of air.

In some remote province,
There lived a poor man
Who kept trying all his life
To master the difficult art.
Finally, one lean day
He summoned his starving family.

His first steps were,
Reputedly,
Only slightly elevated,
But then he rose
Over the huts and trees,
And even the far-off palaces.

High in the sky he floated
Clutching his hat
Among the dragon-tailed,
Razor-studded kites,
On a day, let's say
Just as cold and windy as today.

MIDPOINT

No sooner had I left A.
Than I started doubting its existence:
Its streets and noisy crowds;
Its famous all-night cafes and prisons.

It was dinnertime. The bakeries were closing:
Their shelves empty and white with flour.
The grocers were lowering their iron-grilles.
A lovely young woman was buying the last casaba
    melon.

Even the back alley where I was born
Blurs, dims . . . O rooftops!
Armadas of bedsheets and shirts
In the blustery, crimson dusk . . .

♦

B. at which I am destined
To arrive by and by
Doesn't exist now. Hurriedly
They're building it for my arrival,

And on that day it will be ready:
Its streets and noisy crowds . . .
Even the schoolhouse where I first
Forged my father's signature . . .

Knowing that on the day
Of my departure
It will vanish forever
Just as A. did.

DRAWN TO PERSPECTIVE

On a long block
Along which runs the wall
Of the House of Correction,
Someone has stopped
To holler the name
Of a son or a daughter.

Everything else in the world lies
As if in abeyance:
The warm summer evening;
The kid on roller skates;
The couple about to embrace
At the vanishing point.